Gratitude, My Saviour

(30 days workbook
with
an ultimate guide)

Uma Srikar

Gratitude, My Saviour

ISBN:

Printed in India.

Dedicated to my mother Late Padma Vishwanathan,

an epitome of love, compassion & magnanimity,

exceptionally sweet in talks sprinkled with humor,

an introvert, a dedicated home maker,

my savior at every turn of my life from unfriendly societal norms,

my pride

&

my inspiration.

Introduction

Be the Change you want to see in the World

~ Mahatma Gandhi

As a child, I was extra sensitive. I was fortunate to have a very loving and caring family. They kept my confidence high by appreciating littlest of my achievements. I never got a NO as an answer for whatever I asked for.

I never get to hear what I have to do or say or to behave in a certain way unlike what I usually see around, in other families. Infact, I was highly pampered being the youngest in the family. I cherished all the privileges that my other 2 brothers were showered with.

Their approach not only strengthened our bondings, it also made me very independent. I had a voice in everything that would happen in the house.

Life was simple and people were easygoing.

My mother had a golden heart. A heart full of love and compassion. She had never ever even once scolded any of us, when we were a child.

I have a very high regard for her as she saved me many times from unfriendly societal norms. She gave me a lot of space to err and learn.

I had missed her company badly after my marriage. For many years, we were not in touch. Sometimes, you choose to do certain things you would have never ever thought of doing, due to your own hierarchy of values, you have consciously or unconsciously given your consent to. My topmost value has always been health and peace.

I was exploring the world, all alone, in a new city for few years, then amongst new family set up. And what I realised about the society and people around, wasn't very palatable. I experienced rudeness, irresponsibility, ego-clashes, meaningless power games of worst kind.....And I saw the same scenario, everywhere I went. Everyone looked disturbed, restless and dis-oriented in life. These revelations saddened me further.

I felt there would be a way to make this world more liveable, firstly for me. I felt a missing link, everywhere. Everyone wants to grow yet what they do, is only taking them down, as a human.

Even though cut-throat competitions and unnecessary comparisons push them to perform better and live materialistically more sophisticated lives, yet all look anxious, edgy, worried, unhappy and sad. Even I was pushed into such situations. Not once, but innumerable times. I maintained my calm and gave my best and never compromised on my core values, the topmost being the PEACE within and around.

While on the path of self-discovery during those tough days, I was exposed to the concept of Gratitude. I found the deeply felt missing link to live a good life, in it too. The Gratitude exercises transformed me completely. I was surprised by its simplicity. And the results were very profound. I have been practicing gratitude now for almost 1.5 decades. I experimented with the concept in many ways.

In these Gratitude exercises I saw a solution to combat the constant complaints, which is sandwiched between feelings of lack and feelings of desperation to fill that lack. I came up with free whatsapp workshops as a 30 days Gratitude Challenge for several years under various themes e.g., family, health, relationships, mother, father, spouse, festivals, India, our motherland, and many many more. Their positive and encouraging feedback made me think to take it to more and more people. I was constantly finding ways to do it.

My mother has been my biggest inspiration. I am yet to meet someone who could come even a bit closer to her in matching the love and compassion she had for people around, especially the genuine love and concern she had for me. Unfortunately, she expired on 29th April, 2023. This was a devastating experience for me. I miss her very badly. Her soothing voice, comforting tone, re-assuring talks, loving words, caring gestures and pious attitude is a rare combination that I admire the most. These were like a magic wand. When played on me, it would magically shift my inner state. I would feel grounded instantly. She enriched my life with many such magically humbling moments. Sometimes, I dream of a world, which is full of such pure souls with hearts brimmed with love and compassion. Wouldn't this be heaven on earth, then ?

As an assignment in NLP Train The Transformers Course, we had to choose a niche. And write a book too. My obvious choice was Gratitude.

I have seen people having many questions regarding gratitude, so I thought of creating a short guide book in a question answer format. I have given my best to include all the probable questions a beginner or already practicing seeker may have.

Gratitude in heart, takes you to the state that attracts the BEST for you, and turns your life into magic.

Lets embark on a new journey TOGETHER and create a more COMPASSIONATE WORLD as we evolve more and more, deeper we go into the practice of Gratitude.

Yes, it is possible because....

It is the BETTER VERSION of YOU that creates a BRIGHTER WORLD.

It is the HAPPINESS in YOU that creates a SMILING WORLD.

It is the CONFIDENCE in YOU that creates an EMPOWERING WORLD.

It is the CONTENT in YOU that creates a PEACEFUL WORLD.

It is the GRATEFULNESS in YOU that creates a COMPASSIONATE WORLD.

It all starts with YOU.

It all starts with a single person.

It all starts with SELF.

Lets Re-Design Inner Pathways with Gratitude.

Use this book, share it and spread the word as much as possible.

All the BEST !

Thank you,

Uma Srikar

Founder - Padm-Smriddhi

Acknowledgements

First and foremost, my deepest gratitude to my mother for being the driving force behind every pursuit, including writing this workbook. She expired very recently, ie. on 29th April, 2023. I feel her presence even now. This only helps in keeping myself connected and grounded. Hence, I am fully focussed on the job. Thank you Amma. Thank you. Thank you. Thank you.

My deepest gratitude to my dear husband, Srikar, for extending all kinds of comfort and support, throughtout the duration of the course especially while writing this short guidebook cum workbook. In a world where I hear about financial restrictions after leaving the job, he supported my choice of doing the NLP course. Besides, he extended his helping hand in completing this time-demanding course by adjusting his daily schedules. Without this help, it would have been impossible to even begin the course. Thank you. Thank you. Thank you.

My deepest gratitude to my dear father (he expired in 1986) & brothers, Narayan and Raman, for holding my hands and helping me lay a strong foundation of my personality & outlook, very early in life, through their deep trust, genuine support and concern. Thank you. Thank you. Thank you.

I am immensely grateful to all the teachers in LFH and CHGS, especially primary teachers, who taught me how to read, speak and write in English. Thank you. Thank you. Thank you.

I am extremely grateful and immensely thankful to my mentor Dr. Mehernosh Randheria for teaching not only the ABC of NLP yet also to create curiosity at every step and pushing me one step ahead at a time, towards completing this 2 years long course, on time. And also for always trusting my capability. Thank you Mehernosh Sir. Thank you. Thank you. Thank you.

I am deeply thankful and grateful to Pavan Bhattad Sir for being the catalyst in the journey of learning NLP. His knowledge sharing, quick witted responses, and strict deadlines for assignments had kept us on toes throughout. Thank you Pavan Sir. Thank you. Thank you. Thank you.

Heena Joshi, our book coach as well as our NLP buddy has contributed immensely in getting the nuances of writing a book correctly. Her deeply researched content surely deserves a big applause. Big thanks to dear Heena for being the guiding light in this book writing journey. Thank you Heena. Thank you. Thank you. Thank you.

I am deeply grateful to each and every participant of NLP Practitioners, NLP Masters and TTT programs as I could understand the subject well only because of class discussions from different perspectives, group practice sessions and breakout room sessions. Thank you. Thank you. Thank you.

I am deeply grateful to all the known and unknown people and things around, for giving me opportunities to analyse and apply NLP tools and techniques, and also for enhancing my level of awareness. E.g. laptop (apple), phone (samsung), the internet, network provider (Jio & Vodaphone), the internet connectivity, audios and videos on working condition, swiggy & zomato to come handy on those busy NLP assignment days, calm and quiet environment and many unknown favourable energies around that contributed to complete this course. Thank you. Thank you. Thank you.

A big thanks to all the trials and tribulations in my life since my childhood, as I could work on each of them, use the NLP tools and techniques learnt and understand and see life, people and society in a better perspective. Thanks to each person and every critical scenario that helped me evolve. And thanks to NLP for enriching me with successful mindset principles. Thank you. Thank you. Thank you.

I am deeply thankful to Richard Bandler and John Grinder for co-founding NLP (Neuro Linguistic Programme) and making it available to us in the simplest form. Thank you. Thank you. Thank you.

I am also deeply thankful to all the people who worked in the field of NLP after Richard Bandler and John Grinder and making it simpler and richer with research backed processes. Thank you. Thank you. Thank you.

I am enormously grateful to all the NLP books and their authors for helping us understand the subject in a deeper way with better clarity. Thank you. Thank you. Thank you.

I extend my deeply felt thankfulness to the great creation 'The Magic' and the author Rhonda Byrne. I have read this book many times with a small group of people. Thanks to that group of people too, for energetic participation that helped me go through it again and again. Thank you. Thank you. Thank you.

I am also deeply thankful to myself for choosing this course at the right time (during COVID) and ticking off an item from my bucket list. Learning NLP at the deepest level possible was one of my core desires. I am happy I have completed it. Thank you. Thank you. Thank you.

I am deeply thankful to COVID period, as it is because of COVID that this course was made available to us ONLINE. This enabled me to do it from the comfort of my home, that too at a substantially lower cost. Thank you. Thank you. Thank you.

I am also thankful and grateful to the Universe for all the divine interventions, at the appropriate time and co-creating circumstances to sail through this NLP journey smoothly. Thank you. Thank you. Thank you.

Foreword

If abundance is the lock, gratitude is the key. Uma's interactions with me and in class have always been on the lines of gratitude and it always seemed like that gratitude has become her second language.

I am pleasantly surprised to go through her book manuscript, where she has brought her own personal touch through her real-life story nuggets in her workbook. Her workbook exercises and her life experience unfolded a subtly known yet brushed-under-the-carpet kind of truth to me, i.e 'Gratitude is not an attitude, but a lifestyle.'

I have been attempting her workbook prompts and it is a matter of pride to have participants like her as part of our NLP courses, where gratitude is not just a name, but a priceless skill to inculcate. I wish Uma all the best in her upcoming endeavours in gratitude and many others.

- Dr Mehernosh J Randeria

NLP Master Trainer

W3 Coach

Foreword

If 'Thank You' could speak today, it would have been thanking Uma in real sense for bringing up such a deep and meaningful workbook cum guide on gratitude.

In a world where the word 'Thank You' seems to have lost its identity and significance, this gratitude guide cum workbook by Uma has brought life back to this word.

Uma's personal stories from her childhood are the cherry on the cake to add the much needed depth to this gratitude workbook.

I can also recall the times in our Train the Trainer program, where as a student, she always made sure that she connected anything under the Sun with gratitude and whenever she did that, she proved her mettle of inhaling gratitude deeply in her life.

I wish Uma all the very best for more grateful victories and more victorious attitudes in life.

- Pavan Bhattad

Founder of Knowledge & Karma

Pre-launch Endorsements

There is no better way to make someone happy than to introduce them to the practice of expressing gratitude. This comprehensive guidebook and gratitude workbook is sure to set off waves of joy among its readers.

~ Suma Varughese, ex-editor of Life Positive and Society magazines, a writing coach and author of three books.

This gratitude guide is written in a special flow where you can tap your inner thoughts, express it and create the impact. I liked the sequence in which it is opening the layers of journaling. A simple yet habit forming tactic is the USP. Congratulations Author Uma ! Best wishes for your future writings. Keep it up!

~ Pratibha Kamath,

Founder - Kamath Consultants

Division B Director District 98 Toastmasters International.

A short guide cum workbook on Gratitude Is very much the need of the times. This instils a positive approach to dealing with everyday issues both big and small. A simple and relevant guide to a calm, structured and rewarding everyday life.

~ Dr. Ramchandran,

Neurologist, Chennai

This guidebook cum workbook on Gratitude by Uma Srikarji is an easy to follow book with excellent explanations to know, understand and learn how to express gratitude.

~ Lokman Singh,

Training Entrepreneur

Gratitude is Gracious. Gratitude is the easiest way to be in Abundance. I appreciate this piece of work that will help the learners to feel empowered and successful.

~ Dr Mangesh,

President - Centre for Human Development and Neuro Linguistic Research

---

Gratitude is the most powerful emotion. It heals and keeps us joyful, and the more we practise it the better we get at it. I highly recommend this transformational book to anyone who is on a path of self-healing.

~Dr Nandita Shah, SHARAN (Sanctuary for Health and Reconnection to Animals and Nature), Author of Reversing Diabetes in 21 Days

---

The book written by Uma Srikar on Gratitude is an excellent piece of work which would serve as a practical handbook for anyone who wishes to experience the transformative powers of NLP. The templates and practices are especially easy to adapt and implement. Congratulations!

~ Santosh Ghatpande

Founder- Anahat Music Therapy

Mrs. Uma Srikar's "30 Days workbook on Gratitude with an ultimate guide" is a true gem that has left a lasting impact on my life. What sets this book apart is its innovative approach to making gratitude an integral part of daily life. Mrs. Srikar presents gratitude in such an accessible and practical way that it feels effortless to apply in one's daily routine. Her unique strategies and exercises not only encourage the expression of gratitude but also help in recognizing the beauty in everyday moments. The workbook format is a brilliant addition, offering a structured yet flexible framework for personal growth. Kudos to Mrs. Uma Srikar for creating this inspiring resource!

~ Dr Harshal Sathe

MD, DNB, MNAMS

Assistant Prof. Psychiatry

MGIMS, Sewagram

I have been waiting for a book on gratitude, which is for common people, for a long time. When I see the content of this book, I feel overwhelmed, because everything is written in a very simple way without using any complex terminology. Expression of thought and suggestions are very effective. Best thing is that proper technique is explained to practise gratitude. This book will be really magical for its readers. All the best

~Bharat Kumar,

Founder - IPSTCR (Institute of Psycho Spiritual Therapy, Counselling and Research)

Contents

What am I grateful for today ? (Prompts)

Physical Health Alive Breathing Hands Legs Brain Lungs Kidneys Gallbladder Back Hips Calves Feet Ankles Toes Fingers Wrist Nerves Muscles Bones Blood Mucus Respiratory System Reproductive System Skeleton System Nervous System Circulatory System Excretory System Tooth Mouth Tongue Eyes Face Ears Nose Eyebrows Forehead Hair Nails Neck Fitness Pituitary Pineal Adrenal Energy Hormones Thyroid Stomach Intestines cells organs tendons ligaments blood report vitamins minerals VIT D Vit B12 sunlight walking jogging exercises yoga stretchings water fresh air

Blessings of Health active energetic self dependant support comforts laughter smiles clear vision good hearings walking comfortably hands movement balance

Emotional Health laughter smiles expressions friends family intimacy grief unconditional love care share sadness anger reciprocation acknowledgement feeling heard joy gratitude thankful grateful siblings siblings' love friendship friends friendly behaviours delightful tiredness fatigue stressed out depression peace appreciations togetherness me-time loneliness sleep sleepiness present motherly concern discipline self image self esteem self care time management overwhelm fear worry happiness emotional quotient awareness flexibility stiffness denial rigidity self control

Divine Blessings birth home upbringing parents traditions community childhood experiences coincidences abundance telepathy inborn talents nature planets vastness of sky depth of awareness beauty tonal quality support comforts miracles intuitions magic

Home safety security ceilings furnitures drawing room kitchen guests guestrooms food doors main door locks keys windows mirror bathroom privacy bedroom pillows bed sheets fans ACs window-panes electricity bulbs tube lights kitchen gadgets mixie fridge cups plates storage space storage room cupboard glasses utensils grinder wind chimes decoratives garden plants colours walls curtains warmth togetherness parties get-togethers meals family time own room internet wifi growth cuddles pillow fights kids abundance coffee daal-rice cooking home-cooked relaxation belongings books book-shelf reading corner home-temple taps shower sinks drainage toilet pipes water-supply sunlight air-circulations natural light recycling recycle bin waste bin

Gifts of Nature rainbows rains climate summers winters winter veggies plants trees greenaries waterfalls soothing nurture roots leaves flowers roses lotus water pond water bodies wind sunlight sunshine sky rainbow colours veggies potatoes palak cauliflower carrots beetroots onions bananas fruits pomegranates fruit-meal sprouts lentils rice wheat millets nuts seeds dates prunes walnuts cashews chia seeds fox nuts coconuts spring mountains sunrise sunsets blue sky red sky beauty of dawn breathing mechanism our body different species variety of birds animal kingdom dogs cats pests

Gifts of Science mobile television internet phones telegram weighing scale kitchen gadgets mixie grinder fridge water supply system electricity supply system roads traffic signals sewage system transportations cars bikes buses trains pens computer internet bags flasks bottles gel pens notebooks diaries papers printers bicycle sewing machines pasteurised milk curd maker kitchen appliances fighter planes trucks planes trains metros whatsapp

People / Professionals maids maid servants drivers traffic police policemen soldiers army men navy officers air force crews border security force pilots newspaper vendors waiters chefs gardener photographers shopkeepers grocery keeper sweepers dry cleaners doctors nurses lawyers fashion designers image consultants graphic designers neighbours neighbourhood bankers money lenders friends close friends old friends school friends mother father brother sister uncles aunts kids siblings

Hobbies / entertainments / interests gardening swimming running jogging drawing movies netflix youtube social media facebook twitter youtube videos insta reels table tennis lawn tennis walking marathon reading writing photography teaching Sailing river rafting camping travelling blogging video blogging hiking trekking gymming gyms travelling bags boots cameras teaching tools rackets playgrounds nature walks heritage walks tour guides vacations solo travellings food tasting wine tasting dramatics life-saving jackets history aeronautics photography healings arts group chatting shopping stitching

Foods & Clothings/Accessories favourite meals favourite desserts daal rice chapatis salads juices green juices mangoes oranges watermelons farmers fruitsellers vegetable sellers wholesale markets sabji mandi farmers market cotton silks silkworms chocolates dark chocolates leafy vegetables lettuce pomegranates corn tomatoes lemons moringa leaves sugarcanes sugar salt sea salt sugarcane juice vinegar pickles papads street foods pulao biryani spices peppers capsicums broccoli exotic fruits exotic vegetables grapefruit papaya seasonal fruits favourite snacks seasonal veggies cotton kurta cotton socks kurta salwar kurta dupatta malls online shopping swiggy zomato blinkit meesho bigbasket nyka online stores delivery boy delivery vehicle phone facility shirts pants favourite colours favourite dress pyjamas inners shoes sandals accessories watches rings hair clips hair bands hair cuts salons

Miscellaneous scientists technology memories sense of awareness sense of perception listening human life upskilling mutual respects partnerships confidence sense of right and wrong decisions decision-making capability visions foresight beliefs values opportunities challenges picnics human relations smell of roses smell of perfumes / itr beauty of full moon astrology rishis and munis discoveries discoverers Shankaracharyas writers poets scholars google Steve Jobs Apple android samsung lenovo free workshops udemy coursera free trainings people behind luxuries public transport

Inner Resources courage intuition energy hopeful certainty values beliefs memory recall forgiveness generosity inner calling intelligence divinity perspectives ability to change resilience love understanding power chakras cellular intelligence body intelligence abundance within inner voice mindset attitude reflex actions quick-wittedness choice making instant decisions will power determination compassion

Diabetes insulin blood report glucose pancreas neuropathy eye health feet body weight energy diet exercise sleep Hb1Ac doctor nurses syringe blood pressure blood pressure machine glucose testing tools ICU regular tests hydration sugar sugarless clean food lifestyle walk reversal programs internal organs cells of pancreas liver kidney lungs breathing exercises pranayamas yoga intermittent fasting hormones

Asthma lungs respiratory system trachea nose nasal passage jal neti pranayama inhaler medicines air breathings inhalations exhalations nature walk stress free brain energy oxygen X-rays chest yoga doctor ICU nurses cells mitochondria immunity allergy congestion detox fastings

Heart ailments heart blood circulation veins arteries blockages cholesterol blood report lipid profile RBC WBC haemoglobin triglycerides HDL LDL stress exercise fasting intermittent fasting detox oil free dairy free diet hydration yoga pranayama calm meditation nature walk comedy ICU doctor nurses regular tests blood report rest sleep vacation lifestyle food timings happiness peace calm

Arthritis joints legs toes ankles feet hands arms fingers wrist elbow knees hips body pain energy level sleep pranayama lifestyle yoga therapy physio reports emotions stubbornness stiffness relaxations muscles weights walk nature medicines doctor doctor's visit Vit D3 cells

The Beginning

I hurriedly entered a posh restaurant near the Santa Cruz airport in Mumbai. Neha ran towards me screaming with joy. I too was overjoyed with happiness. We just stood in front of each other, smiling ear to ear. Both went silent. No words were exchanged yet a lot were spoken during those few moments.

Suddenly, I noticed the table Neha came running from. An array of street foods were laid out. I was pleasantly surprised at her thoughtfulness and our good old memories of frequently visiting together the famous 'Kashi Chat Bhandar' at my hometown, Benaras.

This was our meeting after more than a few decades. We studied together in the same school and went to the same University in Banaras Hindu University. Then, parted ways as she chose to marry and settle down at New Delhi and I came to Mumbai to explore my dream life.

Neha, all of a sudden said, 'Uma, you have changed so much ! I just can't believe it.'

'Really ? What changes do you see in me ? Though, it is obvious. It's been a long time now.' I blurted.

'अरे नहीं ! I could recall how serious you were earlier. And you used to only speak about school, college and music. Now, I dont see that anger as well, जो तुम्हारे नाक पर हमेशा चढ़ा रहता था', She smiled.

'Your observations are absolutely right. I am no longer the same person. Got bored one day, so I changed myself upside down. ठीक हैं न ?', I laughed.

'Very funny !! That's ok. Yet curious to know, how come such a huge change happened in your personality ? What did you do ? I heard from Nikita, you practise gratitude and .....and..............I am unable to recall. She mentioned many things, actually. Is that right, what she said ? What are you studying now-a-days ?'

'O yes. It is gratitude. Gratitude practice completely changed my life. Everyone should go for it. It is simple yet very profound.'

'Hey ! Teach me na ! I am interested. Start from the very beginning. Considering that, I know nothing about this field. You said, it is simple so we can start now also. Right ?'

'Absolutely !! Let's do one thing. You ask me questions and I will answer them.'

'Ok. My very first question is ' What is Gratitude ?'

'Well, that will be the first chapter of the book, I am writing on Gratitude.'

Chapter 1. What is Gratitude ?

'What is Gratitude ? Can we get a picture of how it looks like, feels like or sounds like ?'

'Absolutely Yes.'

'Gratitude is what an umbrella is, in summers and winters.

Gratitude is what an ink is, in a pen.

Gratitude is what good content is, to good writing.

Gratitude is what concoction is, in a cup of filter coffee.

Gratitude is what primary colours are, in the colour palette.

Gratitude is what a traffic signal is, on the busy roads.

Gratitude is what Sachin means to Indian Cricket.

Gratitude is what a charger is, to your mobile phone.

Gratitude is what mindfulness is, to a monk.

Gratitude is what a secret ingredient is, in the winner's recipe.

Gratitude is what PRANA is, as you breathe.'

'Did you get it ?'

'Hmmm....'

'Yes, Gratitude is the missing link that connects humans to humanity.'

'Gratitude is that missing link that makes your life WHOLE.

Gratitude is that missing link that helps you recover and regain your HEALTH faster and fully.

Gratitude is that missing link that lets you have HARMONY and PEACE at home.

Gratitude is that missing link that lets you live your life as per your POTENTIAL.

Gratitude is that missing link that accelerates your PROGRESS in every WALKs of your life.

In short, Gratitude is an INSEPARABLE PART of our lives.

Embracing Gratitude is the ONLY WAY to live LIFE to call it THRIVING.'

'Are you ready to infuse this MISSING yet ESSENTIAL INGREDIENT into your LIFE ?'

'Yes, Yes. Yes. Gratitude is the KEY for all kinds of abundance.'

'Aha !! You got that right Neha ! Welcome to the World of Gratitude.'

—xx—

Chapter 2. GRATITUDE - Is saying THANK YOU enough ?

'Arent we all learned to say 'Thank You' when we receive a gift ?' Neha asked.

'Yes. We have.'

' What more to learn about Gratitude, then ? Is it more than saying 'Thank You' ?

'Saying 'Thank You' is one thing. Feeling 'Thankful' is another. And saying 'Thank You' with feelings of thankfulness is how we express Gratitude.

'Aha ! Tell me more. This is interesting.'

'Yes. What we learnt as a child is to say 'Thank You' everytime we get a chocolate from our uncles, neighbours or friends. I could recall how my mother taught me about being thankful. It is a little different. She believed in 'Thanking God' for all the goodness in life. She would tell me to keep the gifts e.g., dresses, jewelleries etc in the home temple. Bow down to the Almighty with folded hands. Or, do Namaskarams (with bent knees, head and hands touching the floor). Once done, I would be rewarded with a 'shamatth kutti' (சமத்த குட்டி in Tamil) means 'good girl', which would sound like a melody of wind chimes that would melt down my heart, eyes would sparkle with joy, and face would illuminate with a joyous, effortless smile. I would crave to hear 'shamatth kutti (சமத்த குட்டி)'. Somehow I would resonate with what I was told to do, as I was sure I would hear my favourite melody 'shamatth kutti (சமத்த குட்டி)' once I completed the task.'

'Yes. I relate with it completely. Do you still follow it ?'

'Sometimes ! And every time I do it, it takes me to those nostalgic days. I feel so grateful within, that immediately, I extend my thankfulness to my mother for enriching me with these 'now least practised' experiences.' I smiled.

'And that's the way to express Gratitude !! Right ?'

'Perfect.' I concluded.

—xx—

Chapter 3 : What do I do when I don't FEEL grateful yet have a reason to express gratitude ?

'As I was entering my parent's home last evening, I was very furious as I was still digesting the words of Shaan. At times, he is so rude to me. The maid at my parents' home was so nice, she smilingly volunteered to extend her work timings, so she could cook my favourite dish. I wanted to thank her, yet my mind was so full of anguish that somehow I could only manage to give her a fake smile. So, how do I express Gratitude in these scenarios?'

'Good question Neha ! At times, we don't feel gratitude yet land up in a situation that demands us to say 'thank you'. This is where our emotional quotient plays a role. How quickly you could switch from one state to another, as needed, determines your level of behavioural flexibility. More flexibility the better is the result.

Imagine, you could have felt gratefulness for your maid at that moment, what would have happened ? How have you behaved ?

'Um....ok. I would have happily rushed to her and hugged her. I would have said 'Thank You' straight from my heart, looking at her beautiful eyes. Afterall, she has her own small kids to attend to yet she decided to wait for an hour more to serve me. I am truly grateful to her.'

'In that case, you should practise doing what you want to do, till you get there where it happens automatically.'

'Means?'

'Yesterday, you would have done the same thing that you explained just now.'

'Without feeling gratefulness ? With those angry feelings deep inside for Shaan ?'

'Yes. Take a note of one more mantra - Fake it till you make it.'

'Oh!'

'Our body and mind are part of the same system. Your gestures, even if fake, towards your maid will have an impact on your psychology as well.

'Hmm.....'

'What you did is also ok. You can do what you want to, I mean hugging her and all, even now. In these scenarios, you may thank a little later, once you settle down with the conflicts within. It all depends on you - how you lead your emotions and feelings.'

'Great point. In a nutshell, I have to improve on my emotional quotient.'

'And it is a process. These situations are opportunities to practise and assess your flexibility.'

'Thank you.'

'Welcome.'

—xx—

Chapter 4 : How can I feel grateful about negative instances in life ?

'Well, I understood that underneath the spoken words "Thank You" there should be feelings as well, of gratefulness. So, here you are saying that what we say, and what we feel, should match. In other words, say it when you feel it. Be authentic"

'O Yes ! You worded that beautifully Neha. This is a practice "to be true to yourself" as well."

'Got it. What if I don't get the feel of gratefulness despite identifying the things I should be. For example, last week I had an argument with my friend, Sumi. When I look back, I feel the entire situation did one good thing to me. I became aware that I should not mess with her because winning an argument with her means you have to have loads of time. She doesn't give up at all. And I don't like to spend soooo much time on one topic. I am ok to agree to disagree. Yet she doesn't budge. This entire episode of yesterday left such a bad taste in my mouth that.......feeling grateful about it ? ah ....How can I ? Is it practical ? How can I feel grateful about this ? I lost 2 hours of my precious life.' Neha's face displayed emotions of anger and confusion.

'I understand your point. You said you became aware of one most important thing about her.'

'Yes. I agree. Surely, I have gained many insights.' Neha looked thoughtful.

'Exactly !! How do you feel now about those precious insights ? Do you think you could get those insights without the process that you went through yesterday ?'

'I think.....(pauses and thinks deeply) nope. Not possible. I have become wiser after that episode.'

'Aha ! Another point you got now.'

'Yet, when I look at the situation, I could recall only her loud voice, frowns and weird gestures that she was making, sitting on that huge blue sofa. How can I feel grateful about those ?'

'You dont have to feel grateful about those things. You CANNOT. Pick the beneficial points and say thanks only for that. It takes time to develop the muscle of gratefulness. To begin with, find the benefits and feel grateful for that. And say 'Thank You'.

'Got it ! अरे ! Hey! Whom to say Thank You, here ?' Neha's eyebrows broadened and eyes widened up.

'That's the topic of the next chapter !' I gave her an assuring smile.

—xx—

Chapter 5 : Who should we say 'Thank you' to ?

'My brother in law feels he made a wrong decision when he decided to quit government job and took up a job in a private bank. Now, reflecting upon what this decision did to him, he regrets a lot. I understand, there were few positives as well. I see those points to feel grateful about. My question is, who should he say 'Thanks' to, here ?'

'Let me dramatise this a bit. Imagine this happened to you. I mean, imagine you were in a government job and you quit the job and all. Now, my question is, who do you think is making you decide that you decide, make you feel that you feel, make you act in a certain way that you act ?'

'Hm........(after a long pause)........I believe in higher forces. They always guide us.

'Ok. Simple. Say 'Thank you' to those higher forces.'

'And there are people who don't believe in higher forces. Then ?' Neha looked concerned.

'Ask them the question that I asked you. If they feel, the entire Universe is residing in them or no one is above them. They may say 'Thank You' to Self.'

'Interesting.'

'Let me add a little more points here. It helps when you are clear about whom you want to Thank or show your gratefulness to. Many believe, it is GOD who is responsible for everything. They may be thankful to God for everything. Some believe in UNIVERSE. They feel, UNIVERSE is the highest authority. Everything is happening to us or by us, because the Universe wants us to do that. So, let them Thank the dear Universe. It all depends on what you believe in. You may say..

Thank you God (you may use your favourite God's or Goddess's name)

Thank you Universe

Thank you Almighty

Thank you Unseen forces.

Thank you my Higher Self.

Thank you Mother Nature.

Thank You Parents / Ancestors.

Thank You Angels.

'Very nice. I love Sai Baba. I will say Thank You Sai Baba.'

'Perfect'

—xx—

Chapter 6 : A short summary of chapter 1- 5

' Let me recall what I learnt so far about Gratitude.'

'Sure. I appreciate the approach. Go on.'

'Thank you. So, I understand that

1. Gratitude is the missing link to having a fulfilling life. Despite doing our BEST, sometimes, we feel we are missing something to reach that DESIRED GOAL or to feel satisfied with LIFE. It could be very well addressed with the practice of Gratitude.
2. Gratitude is nothing but focussing on what we HAVE. We usually take it for granted. Habitually, we focus more on what we DON'T HAVE or WANT to HAVE and keep feeling the lack within since it is out of reach, yet. This is one reason to feel miserable despite having lots in our life.
3. 'Thank You' are the MAGIC WORDS that we use to express our Gratitude.
4. Catch here is to feel the gratitude as deeply as possible while saying 'Thank You'.
5. Expressing Gratitude in a correct way is like a muscle that has to be built up with practice. That's why a daily routine of gratitude practice helps.'

'WOW ! Wonderful job !! You got all the points correctly. Congratulations !!!'

Chapter 7 : Is saying 'Thank You' the only way to express Gratitude ? - Part I.

'Now, my next question is, is saying 'ThankYou' the only way to express Gratitude ?'

'Amazing !! You have asked a very valid question. My answer is NO. I will explain this in 2 parts. Firstly, how have we been doing it as a vedic ritual ? Secondly, 3 ways of expressing Gratitude. So, that will be our next two chapters.'

'That's fine. Thank You. Thank You. Thank You.'

'There are many ways to express Gratitude. You, yourself must have done it innumerable times so far.

Let me remind you. When our uncles or elders come home, is it not expected that you touch their feet and take their blessings? As Indians, at least during my childhood days, I witnessed these in almost every household. Now, definitely, ways have changed. Yet, what is it ? We are expressing our Gratitude to them. But do we feel the gratitude within, nowadays ? I am NOT sure. If both happen simultaneously, surely it is another way to express Gratitude.

We share a deep bonding with family members, from father's side and mother's side. Even genetically we are connected. We are connected with our ancestors too. And how do we express our Gratitude to them ? There are days (shraddha day - श्राद्ध), even a fortnight in a year (Shraddha Paksh - श्राद्ध पक्ष), is dedicated to our ancestors. Through different vedic rituals we pay our respects to them. We do it with loads of respect in our hearts for them. They call it 'Shraddha - श्रद्धा'. This is nothing but expressing our Gratitude.

We all carry a part of our ancestors with us. Sometimes, our face, nose, eyebrows, forehead, tone, words, attitude reminds us of maternal or paternal uncle, aunty, grandparents or great grandparents, to many. Isnt it ?

By expressing Gratitude to them, we only express Gratitude to that PART in us, that we carry all the time.'

'Mind Blowing ! There is so much about Gratitude ! And it is so very important to be grateful even to our ancestors !! I never thought in this line.'

'You are right. Now, in modern days, when people are blindly following modern ways of living, touching feet of elders or doing vedic rituals are not to be seen around, most often. So, these gratitude exercises are surely a SAVIOUR to NOT miss out on the essence or benefits.'

'Thank you. Thank you. Thank you. I am loving this journey of exploring the Gratitude practices. Please carry on. '

'They say, 'Shrddha - श्रद्धा' in following the Vedic Rituals has gone down. Glad to know you are loving this journey. By the way, it is my habit to say 'Thank You' 3 times, the way you just said. I feel more connected when I say it 3 times'

'Wonderful !! Looks like I am getting aligned with your knowledge sharing and somewhere tapping on your consciousness. Am I ? What do you think ?'

'Very much possible. We all model each other, all the time. Kids are the BEST example for this. How do they copy the gestures and words of people around them ? They model them unconsciously. You are aware. That's nice'.

—xx—

Chapter 8 : Is saying 'Thank You' the only way to express Gratitude ? - Part II

'Let me share other ways to express gratitude.

Appreciation - with gestures. When I topped the school in my 10th std, I was poured with appreciation from everybody. Few used the words ie. वाह! कमाल कर दिया तुमने ! (You did it !!) And few kept looking at me, their hearts brimming with pride and appreciation for me, eyes moistened with happiness and a big, broad, effortless smile. They were so overwhelmed with the news that words were not coming out of their mouths. We all were in the same zone. SILENTLY appreciating each other and celebrating the JOY. Just then, my mother said 'God is Great !! Thanks to HIM.'

Yes. We left no one, at that time, to acknowledge their contribution to our JOY.'

Acknowledgement : with a thankful heart. Acknowledge other's contribution for the JOY or overall well-being whenever you realise it. This is another way to express Gratitude. Again, you need not use words. I went to a few of my teachers' homes with sweets, sat with them, and spent some time. Being very introverted and shy during those days, I hardly spoke. I would only say a word or a line as an answer. Yet they knew what I am there for and blessed me magnanimously. It is all about what you are comfortable with or your style of acknowledgement.

Well, tell me, who is your favourite fashion model or movie star ?'

'Salman Khan. No doubt !! He does so much charity under 'Being Human'. I love that about him'

'What do you do special for Salman that you don't do for any other movie star ?'

'I watch all his movies. I absolutely don't miss that. I keep saying 'I love you' everytime he comes on screen or I like any of his punch lines or dancing moves. And.....'

'Ok. Ok. Ok...got it. So, you reciprocate this way for how he makes you feel good within. This is also a way to express Gratitude. Just be aware of the entire process.

Admiration : with a curious and happy heart. This is another way to express Gratitude. You express Gratitude NOT only for tangible things but also for richness in feelings that adds to your overall well being. When you see someone ahead of you in any field and you feel inspired by that, you may simply ask, " How do you do that ?" '

'Wow !! That's a nice revelation ! How do YOU do that ?'

'Haha....You are very quick at grasping. Thank You. Thank You. Thank You.'

Chapter 9 : Benefits of Gratitude

'I understand now, the importance of Gratitude as the missing link to the desired goal. Could you elaborate more on how we benefit when we are in the state of Gratitude ?'

'Absolutely. Benefits of being in a thankful state are countless. Let me share a few of them.

1. In this state of gratitude you are deeply connected with SELF.
2. You make BEST choices and make RIGHT decisions. (diets, exercises, hobbies)
3. Your self worth increases. You feel good about yourself and your life.
4. Your confidence improves.
5. Your social circle expands. Who doesn't want to be around happy people ?
6. Your head is clutter free and this helps you focus on what really matters.
7. Gratitude is also the missing link in the law of attraction. Now, you will attract more of what you truly deserve.
8. You will feel fulfilled. You will feel your life is WHOLE.
9. Your energy level will dramatically improve.
10. Your immune system will improve.
11. Your body will listen to you more.

12. You will become the source of spreading joy and happiness.

13. You will recover from setbacks faster.

14. Situations in life can not knock you down easily.

15. You have a sound sleep.

16. You become generous & kinder even to unknown people.

'Wow ! That's a big list of benefits. And you said, there are countless benefits.'

'Yes. Countless for sure. Imagine the domino's effect of the benefits I have mentioned above. Our mind and body are connected. So are our different areas of life. A little change in one segment will bring changes in many other aspects of our life. Hence, countless benefits.'

'Fantastic. Thank you for that rich sharing. Thank you. Thank you. Thank you.'

'Welcome. And Thank you.'

—xx—

Chapter 10 : Gratitude and Money

'Just curious ! What is the impact of Gratitude in money matters ?'

'Aha ! Money is an essential thing in our life. Good you asked this question. Many work very hard, yet don't see much money in their life. The reason may lie on what thoughts they entertain 24x7 about money. Nobody wants to come near you, if you don't give importance. You may work very hard to earn. Yet deep down you may have negative beliefs about Money that may be stopping you from getting what you truly deserve.'

'You mean our beliefs matter ?'

'Ofcourse !!

Many of us absorb many beliefs about money as a child, from people around us. Let me give some examples that you must have heard from your grandparents or parents as a child.

1. You have to work HARD to earn good money.
2. Money is the root of all human conflicts.
3. Money is evil.
4. It is OK if you don't have much money. Don't be greedy.
5. Relationships are more important than Money.

In all these statements, you can clearly see how valuations of Money is degraded. These cannot be beliefs about Money of rich people.

Once you develop the attitude of gratitude and see everything about yourself including your beliefs from the lens of Gratitude, you get a different perspective and you loosen up on these beliefs as you become more and more aware of these limiting beliefs.

Gratitude is the mindset of Abundance. There will be no space to fill with anything that would limit you once you adopt this mindset.

Hope this helps.'

'O Yes. Very very much. Thank You. Thank You. Thank You. Gratitude attracts an abundance of money as well. Wow ! That sounds so good.'

'Thank You. Glad you loved it Neha.'

—xx—

Chapter 11 : Gratitude and The Law of Attraction

'How will you relate these Gratitude exercises with Law of Attractions ?'

'Law of attraction is all about attracting whatever frequency you are vibrating with. Every emotion is given a frequency. Being in a grateful state will enhance your chances to attract more of what you may feel grateful about. Isnt it wonderful ?'

'I completely agree. Could you elaborate on the frequency and emotions part please ?'

'Let me share a chart with you.'

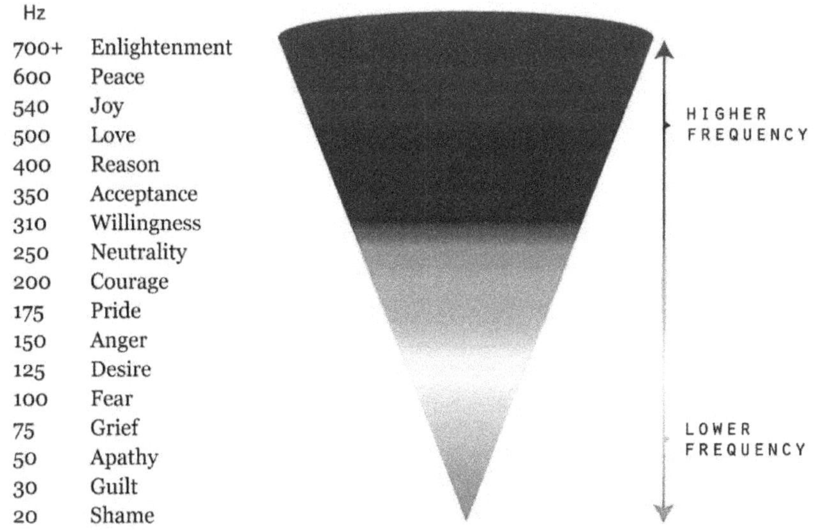

Courtesy : Internet.

Frequency of Gratitude is quoted as 540 MHz. It is the same as the frequency of Joy as you could see in the chart. Practice of Gratitude will propel you from wherever you are to the frequency of 540 MHz.

As per Law of Attraction, you will then attract whatever you will feel more grateful about. Your Joys will only keep multiplying.

'Ahan ! Wow Wow Wow !! I am speechless'

'There is absolutely no reason, one COULD AFFORD to NOT do Gratitude exercises. Agree ?'

'100%. Salute to you for bringing this awareness to me.'

'Thank You. Thank You. Thank You.'

—xx—

Chapter 12 : How to use this guide cum workbook for 30 days ?

'Now that I am very very clear about everything related to Gratitude. Where do I start from ? And how often should I do the exercises ?'

'Well, you may use this workbook as a starting point. There are very few questions under the morning routine and evening routine. When you read the question, go deep within, observe what pops up and just write that. 5mins in the morning and 5mins in the evening (preferably before going to bed).'

'Is that enough ?'

'I have kept it simple for absolute beginners. There are few pages dedicated to prompts. Use that while doing these routines, as well.'

'Please please explain more about these. How to use these prompts ?'

'There are spaces to write what do you feel grateful about and why. Please attempt to write different points every time you do this exercise. To help you come up with different points on different areas, I have listed down around 900+ prompts. You will never go short of topics to feel grateful about.

You may use this Gratitude Workbook in many ways.

1. Go as guided on every page. And fill the spaces given to you. (General Use)

2. In case you have any health issues, use the same workbook and focus on your health issues and come up with things that you feel grateful about. (Current moods/bodily discomforts)

   For example, you have a headache.

   Write everything related to the head that you feel grateful about. You may write..

   I am deeply grateful that my head is coordinating with all other organs vey well and keeping me active.

3. Suppose you are not happy in any relationship, and want to bring improvement. (Relationship Issues) Use this book and focus only on that particular relationship. And write things that you feel grateful about. Also attempt other parts similarly.

   For example, You fought with your husband yesterday. And it is keeping you upset and anxious, even now. You may go back to days, when things were beautiful between you two and write what those moments have added to enhance your well being.

   You may write...

   I am deeply grateful to my husband for those initial days, when I could hardly express myself. He helped me come out of my cocoon.

4. You may use it in case you have been diagnosed with any diseases. For example,

   Diabetes, Asthma, Heart issues....etc. (Illness)

Here, focus on those organs, systems, glands, etc around which this disease has its impact For example, incase of a Heart patients who had survived the heart attack...you may write,

I am deeply grateful that my heart works efficiently and works without any break 24x7 just for me. I am deeply touched and love its dedication towards my well being.

Be creative and come up with points that sound true to you and pour out your true feelings and emotions.

5. Use your creativity and come up with your own ideas to use it for any of your desired goals.

It is all up to you. I have shared only a few ways to use it.'

'Thank you so much. I got a good clarity on how to use it. My question now is what if I miss a day ?'

'Go with the flow. You won't miss a day once you start doing it. I am confident about it. And the reason is the results that you would get just by doing it once. Who doesn't want to be in a good zone ? You will crave to come back and do the exercises again the next day.'

'Despite this, if you miss, don't beat yourself for it. It is ok. Do it when you can recall. Early morning routine if you missed, then do it in the afternoon. Next day, come back to your usual routine. Be flexible. Soon, you will get into the routines. Afterall, this journal is to be used just for 5 mins in the morning and 5 mins in the evening.'

'Got it. Thank you.'

'Now, it's time. Get started. And incase you still have anything to ask, you may contact me on my Whatsapp number 7506880129

Email Id umasrikar741@gmail.com

You are also welcome to share your feedback about this guide cum workbook. How has it improved your quality of life ? I am curious to know.

Thank You. Thank You. Thank You.'

'A big thanks to you Uma. I will surely be in touch with you. चलो, it's time. I have to catch my flight back to New Delhi. It was a very very productive meeting '

'Thank you Neha ! As usual, we had a good conversation. Thanks for a great time. See you soon ! Bye !'

—xx—

Chapter 13 : Gratitude and NLP

Neuro Linguistic Programming is nothing but the study of what works. Gratitude works. It has been scientifically proven.

Let's look at the NLP tools and techniques that support the experience of Gratitude.

1. NLP talks about a principle...

   Mind and Body are part of the same system.

   Or

   Physiology impacts psychology and vice versa.

   When we feel gratitude deeply in our body, it impacts the mind as well.

   So, we may say,

   Gratitude practice leads to mental well being.

2. NLP also talks about FRAMES. And one of them is APPRECIATIVE FRAME which is nothing but being in a state of appreciation.

   Appreciation is one of the ways to express Gratitude.

   Being curious to know what the other person is good at and then instantly appreciating them, takes us to the state of Gratitude.

3. Value elicitation is a part of NLP where we decipher our hierarchy of values. One of the values that people have is 'Happiness'.

   Nothing leads to happiness but a grateful heart. Practising gratitude itself could take a person to a state of happiness with whatever a person has or a person is, right now. It multiplies when we acknowledge its presence in our life, genuinely.

   More Gratitude practices → More Happiness within → Attract More reasons to feel Happy → Feel More Gratitude

   This is how we manifest all the things that make us happy.

   Happiness keeps multiplying.

4. Acknowledging the presence of goodness in our lives is what Gratitude is all about. And acknowledgement happens as we constantly remain aware of these goodness. This enhances our sense of awareness. Awareness is one of the pillars of NLP.

   By practising gratitude we focus and become more and more aware of all of God's Grace. Then, we acknowledge it by deeply feeling thankfulness. This also enhances our level of awareness, which is one of the benefits of NLP tools and techniques.

5. In the process of practising Gratitude we bring in behavioural flexibility to find the reasons to be grateful for, even in the least probable scenarios.

   What we do here is build better rapport with the situations and people involved. We do this within ourselves and practise more flexibility keeping the desired outcome in mind.

Gratitude practice is very much a part of NLP.

Chapter 14 - Gratitude, my life, my practices

My life became very different post landing in Mumbai and changed furthermore after marriage, as I was triggered to question the logic behind all the traditional practices that I was fond of.

I took it as an opportunity to bring tradition and science together. I could see basic human needs beneath most of the traditional practices and also I could see through the distortions it had undergone with time. This made me question the relevance of many of the practices in current time.

For example, we as humans are social beings. It is our need to be in constant touch with other humans and be in cordial relations. These 'connections' and 'bondings' are promoted through our frequent festivals and celebrations that India is popular for. Things happening around this need (going for navratri shopping with friends, playing dandia, setting up a huge pandal for Durga Pooja, ...) is just to create an environment to let these 'connections' happen smoothly and at a deeper level.

Instead, at many occasions, I see people fighting over the ways rituals are to be conducted, or taking pride in their style and feeling down about other groups of people following a different set of rituals. By doing this, we don't bring humans together, we only create differences amongst humans leading to 'feeling disconnected'. This not only leaves a very bad taste in our mouth but also harms the humans & humanity at a deeper level. It creates a huge void in us.

This change in perspective didn't happen overnight. I went through a roller coaster ride as these traditional practices were deeply ingrained in me. Though I was never forced to practise and never did it myself much yet I had a strong belief in these practices. Inner turmoil took a toll on my physical health as well for many many years, as I was tightly holding on to the old beliefs system despite having all the reasons to let it go. I was in an identity crisis. I felt these beliefs are my identity, my roots. And this pushed me into survival mode. Those days, I wasn't aware what was going on within me and how to tackle it.

My entire inner world was demolished at one point of time, which I was very fond of or say, habituated to, knowingly or unknowingly. It wasn't an easy period. This was the time, when every relationship in my life was drastically severed. People gave me suspicious looks, anywhere I went to. I felt like an alien. There was a cold war. Between me and rest of the world. That's how I perceived it at that time.

Thanks to the world of social media. I came across many supportive facebook groups who discuss these kinds of issues. And also offer solutions in terms of changing the mindsets. My journey to bring things in order within me, started from here.

I understood, I have to work on myself and re-design the inner pathways and recreate a beautiful landscape in a way that makes me feel 'at home' with a new set of belief systems, habits, mindsets, routines etc.

This was the time, 'practice of Gratitude' came into my life. I took stock of what I have. I realised that even if my relationships are shattered, I have beautiful memories from our past with them, to cherish. And cherish it not once but again and again. And this is what I started doing.

With regular practice I found that the friction against the same people, within me, drastically reduced and gradually it turned to zero. I could successfully think of all the people, despite any kind of experiences with them, with a grateful heart for whatever goodness they added in my life whether it was a small contribution or a big contribution, whether for a shorter period of time or a longer period. What mattered was how the presence of that person enhanced the quality of my well being. It worked. It worked as a magic wand. Everything looked beautiful.

Daily Gratitude meditation helped me create a calm and quiet place within the landscape that I now go to, every now and then that brings peace and joy in me.

This was my journey with Gratitude exercises.

I also found the book 'The Magic' by Rhonda Byrne very useful as it added many more ways to count on blessings. Deeply thankful.

Thank you. Thank you. Thank you. For reading my story.

Now, it is your turn to follow the workbook and invite magic in your life.

All the Best.

Gratitude !!

—xx—

G-row with Gratitude

R-egularity is the key

A-ppreciate Self, Others & things around

T-ime and space is not a constraint

I-t is an attitude, you develop with practice

T-otally worth it, soon you too will realise

U-nderstand, this is the missing link to manifestation

D-ream life will no more be out of reach

E-mbark on your new journey with "Gratitude, my saviour".

Gratitude Workbook

Day 1 to Day 30

Day 1 (Morning) Date: Time:

A. How grateful are you right now ? (Use a colour pen/pencil of your choice and colour the appropriate box below.

0	1	2	3	4	5	6	7	8	9	10

Do all the exercises below with a broad SMILE on your face.

Close your eyes and scan through your body, mentally - 5 secs.

Open your eyes. Take a coloured pen of your choice and start writing.

I am super excited to start my day because

3 things I feel deeply grateful for, right now, are (write reason as well)

Describe 1 thing from yesterday, that you feel most grateful about Why it is number 1 thing to be grateful about ?

B. How grateful are you right now ?

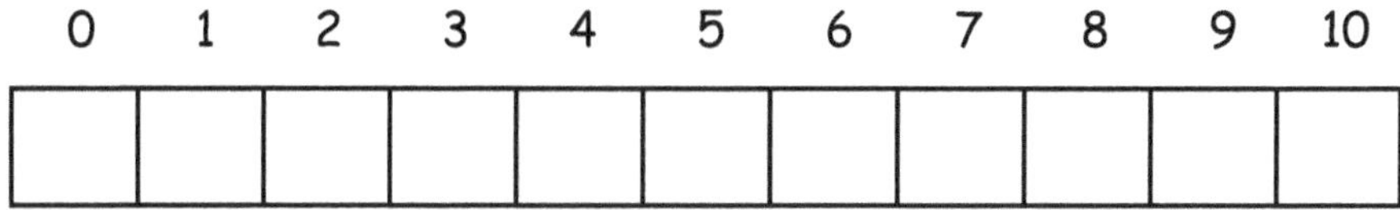

Increase in Gratitude Quotient (B - A) =

"You have no cause for anything but gratitude and joy."

- Buddha

Day 1 (Evening) Date: Time:

A. How grateful are you right now ? (Use colour pen of your choice and colour the appropriate box)

0	1	2	3	4	5	6	7	8	9	10

Take 3 deep breathes with closed eyes and one hand on your chest and another on your belly.

Now, think of any one thing that you feel grateful about. (You may pick a topic from the prompts given in page 5.) And write at length why you are grateful for this. (put a timer for 5mins)

B. How grateful are you right now ? (Use colour pen of your choice and colour the appropriate box)

0	1	2	3	4	5	6	7	8	9	10

Increase in Gratitude Quotient (B - A) =

"You have no cause for anything but gratitude and joy."

- Buddha

Day 2 (Morning) Date: Time:

A. How grateful are you right now ? (Use a colour pen/pencil of your choice and colour the appropriate box below.

0	1	2	3	4	5	6	7	8	9	10

Do all the exercises below with a broad SMILE on your face.

Close your eyes and scan through your body, mentally - 5 secs.

Open your eyes. Take a coloured pen of your choice and start writing.

I am super excited to start my day because

3 things I feel deeply grateful for, right now, are (write reason as well)

Describe 1 thing from yesterday, that you feel most grateful about Why it is number 1 thing to be grateful about ?

B. How grateful are you right now ?

0	1	2	3	4	5	6	7	8	9	10

Increase in Gratitude Quotient (B - A) =

"To be thankful for one thing is infinitely more powerful than to be bitter about a hundred others."

— Craig D. Lounsbrough

Day 2 (Evening)   Date: Time:

A. How grateful are you right now ? (Use colour pen of your choice and colour the appropriate box)

0	1	2	3	4	5	6	7	8	9	10

Take 3 deep breathes with closed eyes and one hand on your chest and another on your belly.

Now, think of any one thing that you feel grateful about. (You may pick a topic from the prompts given in page 5.) And write at length why you are grateful for this. (put a timer for 5mins)

B. How grateful are you right now ? (Use colour pen of your choice and colour the appropriate box)

0	1	2	3	4	5	6	7	8	9	10

Increase in Gratitude Quotient (B - A) =

"To be thankful for one thing is infinitely more powerful than to be bitter about a hundred others."

— Craig D. Lounsbrough

Day 3 (Morning) Date: Time:

A. How grateful are you right now ? (Use a colour pen/pencil of your choice and colour the appropriate box below.

0	1	2	3	4	5	6	7	8	9	10

Do all the exercises below with a broad SMILE on your face.

Close your eyes and scan through your body, mentally - 5 secs.

Open your eyes. Take a coloured pen of your choice and start writing.

I am super excited to start my day because

3 things I feel deeply grateful for, right now, are (write reason as well)

Describe 1 thing from yesterday, that you feel most grateful about Why it is number 1 thing to be grateful about ?

B. How grateful are you right now ?

0	1	2	3	4	5	6	7	8	9	10

Increase in Gratitude Quotient (B - A) =

"Reflect upon your present blessings, of which every man has plenty; not on your past misfortunes, of which all men have some."

- Charles Dickens

Day 3 (Evening) Date: Time:

A. How grateful are you right now ? (Use colour pen of your choice and colour the appropriate box)

0	1	2	3	4	5	6	7	8	9	10

Take 3 deep breathes with closed eyes and one hand on your chest and another on your belly.

Now, think of any one thing that you feel grateful about. (You may pick a topic from the prompts given in page 5.) And write at length why you are grateful for this. (put a timer for 5mins)

B. How grateful are you right now ? (Use colour pen of your choice and colour the appropriate box)

0	1	2	3	4	5	6	7	8	9	10

Increase in Gratitude Quotient (B - A) =

"Reflect upon your present blessings, of which every man has plenty; not on your past misfortunes, of which all men have some."

- Charles Dickens

Day 4 (Morning) Date: Time:

A. How grateful are you right now ? (Use a colour pen/pencil of your choice and colour the appropriate box below.

0	1	2	3	4	5	6	7	8	9	10

Do all the exercises below with a broad SMILE on your face.

Close your eyes and scan through your body, mentally - 5 secs.

Open your eyes. Take a coloured pen of your choice and start writing.

I am super excited to start my day because

3 things I feel deeply grateful for, right now, are (write reason as well)

Describe 1 thing from yesterday, that you feel most grateful about Why it is number 1 thing to be grateful about ?

B. How grateful are you right now ?

0	1	2	3	4	5	6	7	8	9	10

Increase in Gratitude Quotient (B - A) =

"When eating bamboo sprouts, remember the man who planted them."
- Chinese Proverb

Day 4 (Evening) Date: Time:

A. How grateful are you right now ? (Use colour pen of your choice and colour the appropriate box)

0	1	2	3	4	5	6	7	8	9	10

Take 3 deep breathes with closed eyes and one hand on your chest and another on your belly.

Now, think of any one thing that you feel grateful about. (You may pick a topic from the prompts given in page 5.) And write at length why you are grateful for this. (put a timer for 5mins)

B. How grateful are you right now ? (Use colour pen of your choice and colour the appropriate box)

0	1	2	3	4	5	6	7	8	9	10

Increase in Gratitude Quotient (B - A) =

"When eating bamboo sprouts, remember the man who planted them."

- Chinese Proverb

Day 5 (Morning) Date: Time:

A. How grateful are you right now ? (Use a colour pen/pencil of your choice and colour the appropriate box below.

0	1	2	3	4	5	6	7	8	9	10

Do all the exercises below with a broad SMILE on your face.

Close your eyes and scan through your body, mentally - 5 secs.

Open your eyes. Take a coloured pen of your choice and start writing.

I am super excited to start my day because

3 things I feel deeply grateful for, right now, are (write reason as well)

Describe 1 thing from yesterday, that you feel most grateful about Why it is number 1 thing to be grateful about ?

B. How grateful are you right now ?

0	1	2	3	4	5	6	7	8	9	10

Increase in Gratitude Quotient (B - A) =

"Expressing gratitude seems like a cosmic invitation for all kinds of thankfulness and appreciation to pour in."

- Mary Anne Radmacher

Day 5 (Evening)   Date: Time:

A. How grateful are you right now ? (Use colour pen of your choice and colour the appropriate box)

0	1	2	3	4	5	6	7	8	9	10

Take 3 deep breathes with closed eyes and one hand on your chest and another on your belly.

Now, think of any one thing that you feel grateful about. (You may pick a topic from the prompts given in page 5.) And write at length why you are grateful for this. (put a timer for 5mins)

B. How grateful are you right now ? (Use colour pen of your choice and colour the appropriate box)

0	1	2	3	4	5	6	7	8	9	10

Increase in Gratitude Quotient (B - A) =

"Expressing gratitude seems like a cosmic invitation for all kinds of thankfulness and appreciation to pour in."

- Mary Anne Radmacher

Day 6 (Morning) Date: Time:

A. How grateful are you right now ? (Use a colour pen/pencil of your choice and colour the appropriate box below.

0	1	2	3	4	5	6	7	8	9	10

Do all the exercises below with a broad SMILE on your face.

Close your eyes and scan through your body, mentally - 5 secs.

Open your eyes. Take a coloured pen of your choice and start writing.

I am super excited to start my day because

3 things I feel deeply grateful for, right now, are (write reason as well)

Describe 1 thing from yesterday, that you feel most grateful about Why it is number 1 thing to be grateful about ?

B. How grateful are you right now ?

0	1	2	3	4	5	6	7	8	9	10

Increase in Gratitude Quotient (B - A) =

"Begin with praise and honest appreciation."

- Dale Carnegie

Day 6 (Evening) Date: Time:

A. How grateful are you right now ? (Use colour pen of your choice and colour the appropriate box)

0	1	2	3	4	5	6	7	8	9	10

Take 3 deep breathes with closed eyes and one hand on your chest and another on your belly.

Now, think of any one thing that you feel grateful about. (You may pick a topic from the prompts given in page 5.) And write at length why you are grateful for this. (put a timer for 5mins)

B. How grateful are you right now ? (Use colour pen of your choice and colour the appropriate box)

0	1	2	3	4	5	6	7	8	9	10

Increase in Gratitude Quotient (B - A) =

"Begin with praise and honest appreciation."

- Dale Carnegie

Day 7 (Morning) Date: Time:

A. How grateful are you right now ? (Use a colour pen/pencil of your choice and colour the appropriate box below.

0	1	2	3	4	5	6	7	8	9	10

Do all the exercises below with a broad SMILE on your face.

Close your eyes and scan through your body, mentally - 5 secs.

Open your eyes. Take a coloured pen of your choice and start writing.

I am super excited to start my day because

3 things I feel deeply grateful for, right now, are (write reason as well)

Describe 1 thing from yesterday, that you feel most grateful about Why it is number 1 thing to be grateful about ?

B. How grateful are you right now ?

0	1	2	3	4	5	6	7	8	9	10

Increase in Gratitude Quotient (B - A) =

"Gratitude is the most exquisite form of courtesy."

- Jacques Maritain

Day 7 (Evening) Date: Time:

A. How grateful are you right now ? (Use colour pen of your choice and colour the appropriate box)

0	1	2	3	4	5	6	7	8	9	10

Take 3 deep breathes with closed eyes and one hand on your chest and another on your belly.

Now, think of any one thing that you feel grateful about. (You may pick a topic from the prompts given in page 5.) And write at length why you are grateful for this. (put a timer for 5mins)

B. How grateful are you right now ? (Use colour pen of your choice and colour the appropriate box)

0	1	2	3	4	5	6	7	8	9	10

Increase in Gratitude Quotient (B - A) =

"Gratitude is the most exquisite form of courtesy."

- Jacques Maritain

Day 8 (Morning) Date: Time:

A. How grateful are you right now ? (Use a colour pen/pencil of your choice and colour the appropriate box below.

0	1	2	3	4	5	6	7	8	9	10

Do all the exercises below with a broad SMILE on your face.

Close your eyes and scan through your body, mentally - 5 secs.

Open your eyes. Take a coloured pen of your choice and start writing.

I am super excited to start my day because

3 things I feel deeply grateful for, right now, are (write reason as well)

Describe 1 thing from yesterday, that you feel most grateful about Why it is number 1 thing to be grateful about ?

B. How grateful are you right now ?

0	1	2	3	4	5	6	7	8	9	10

Increase in Gratitude Quotient (B - A) =

"Showing gratitude is one of the simplest yet most powerful things humans can do for each other."

- Randy Rausch

Day 8 (Evening) Date: Time:

A. How grateful are you right now ? (Use colour pen of your choice and colour the appropriate box)

0	1	2	3	4	5	6	7	8	9	10

Take 3 deep breathes with closed eyes and one hand on your chest and another on your belly.

Now, think of any one thing that you feel grateful about. (You may pick a topic from the prompts given in page 5.) And write at length why you are grateful for this. (put a timer for 5mins)

B. How grateful are you right now ? (Use colour pen of your choice and colour the appropriate box)

0	1	2	3	4	5	6	7	8	9	10

Increase in Gratitude Quotient (B - A) =

"Showing gratitude is one of the simplest yet most powerful things humans can do for each other."

- Randy Rausch

Day 9 (Morning) Date: Time:

A. How grateful are you right now ? (Use a colour pen/pencil of your choice and colour the appropriate box below.

0	1	2	3	4	5	6	7	8	9	10

Do all the exercises below with a broad SMILE on your face.

Close your eyes and scan through your body, mentally - 5 secs.

Open your eyes. Take a coloured pen of your choice and start writing.

I am super excited to start my day because

3 things I feel deeply grateful for, right now, are (write reason as well)

Describe 1 thing from yesterday, that you feel most grateful about Why it is number 1 thing to be grateful about ?

B. How grateful are you right now ?

0	1	2	3	4	5	6	7	8	9	10

Increase in Gratitude Quotient (B - A) =

"If you are really thankful, what do you do? You share."
— W. Clement Stone

Day 9 (Evening) Date: Time:

A. How grateful are you right now ? (Use colour pen of your choice and colour the appropriate box)

0	1	2	3	4	5	6	7	8	9	10

Take 3 deep breathes with closed eyes and one hand on your chest and another on your belly.

Now, think of any one thing that you feel grateful about. (You may pick a topic from the prompts given in page 5.) And write at length why you are grateful for this. (put a timer for 5mins)

B. How grateful are you right now ? (Use colour pen of your choice and colour the appropriate box)

0	1	2	3	4	5	6	7	8	9	10

Increase in Gratitude Quotient (B - A) =

"If you are really thankful, what do you do? You share."
— W. Clement Stone

Day 10 (Morning) Date: Time:

A. How grateful are you right now ? (Use a colour pen/pencil of your choice and colour the appropriate box below.

0	1	2	3	4	5	6	7	8	9	10

Do all the exercises below with a broad SMILE on your face.

Close your eyes and scan through your body, mentally - 5 secs.

Open your eyes. Take a coloured pen of your choice and start writing.

I am super excited to start my day because

3 things I feel deeply grateful for, right now, are (write reason as well)

Describe 1 thing from yesterday, that you feel most grateful about Why it is number 1 thing to be grateful about ?

B. How grateful are you right now ?

0	1	2	3	4	5	6	7	8	9	10

Increase in Gratitude Quotient (B - A) =

"What you focus on expands, and when you focus on the goodness in your life, you create more of it. Opportunities, relationships, even money flowed my way when I learned to be grateful no matter what happened in my life."

- Oprah Winfrey

Day 10 (Evening) Date: Time:

A. How grateful are you right now ? (Use colour pen of your choice and colour the appropriate box)

0	1	2	3	4	5	6	7	8	9	10

Take 3 deep breathes with closed eyes and one hand on your chest and another on your belly.

Now, think of any one thing that you feel grateful about. (You may pick a topic from the prompts given in page 5.) And write at length why you are grateful for this. (put a timer for 5mins)

B. How grateful are you right now ? (Use colour pen of your choice and colour the appropriate box)

0	1	2	3	4	5	6	7	8	9	10

Increase in Gratitude Quotient (B - A) =

"What you focus on expands, and when you focus on the goodness in your life, you create more of it. Opportunities, relationships, even money flowed my way when I learned to be grateful no matter what happened in my life."

- Oprah Winfrey

Day 11 (Morning) Date: Time:

A. How grateful are you right now ? (Use a colour pen/pencil of your choice and colour the appropriate box below.

0	1	2	3	4	5	6	7	8	9	10

Do all the exercises below with a broad SMILE on your face.

Close your eyes and scan through your body, mentally - 5 secs.

Open your eyes. Take a coloured pen of your choice and start writing.

I am super excited to start my day because

3 things I feel deeply grateful for, right now, are (write reason as well)

Describe 1 thing from yesterday, that you feel most grateful about Why it is number 1 thing to be grateful about ?

B. How grateful are you right now ?

0	1	2	3	4	5	6	7	8	9	10

Increase in Gratitude Quotient (B - A) =

"Gratitude is a mark of a noble soul and a refined character. We like to be around those who are grateful."

- Joseph B. Wirthlin

Day 11 (Evening)   Date: Time:

A. How grateful are you right now ? (Use colour pen of your choice and colour the appropriate box)

0	1	2	3	4	5	6	7	8	9	10

Take 3 deep breathes with closed eyes and one hand on your chest and another on your belly.

Now, think of any one thing that you feel grateful about. (You may pick a topic from the prompts given in page 5.) And write at length why you are grateful for this. (put a timer for 5mins)

B. How grateful are you right now ? (Use colour pen of your choice and colour the appropriate box)

0	1	2	3	4	5	6	7	8	9	10

Increase in Gratitude Quotient (B - A) =

"Gratitude is a mark of a noble soul and a refined character. We like to be around those who are grateful."

- Joseph B. Wirthlin

Day 12 (Morning) Date: Time:

A. How grateful are you right now ? (Use a colour pen/pencil of your choice and colour the appropriate box below.

0	1	2	3	4	5	6	7	8	9	10

Do all the exercises below with a broad SMILE on your face.

Close your eyes and scan through your body, mentally - 5 secs.

Open your eyes. Take a coloured pen of your choice and start writing.

I am super excited to start my day because

3 things I feel deeply grateful for, right now, are (write reason as well)

Describe 1 thing from yesterday, that you feel most grateful about Why it is number 1 thing to be grateful about ?

B. How grateful are you right now ?

0	1	2	3	4	5	6	7	8	9	10

Increase in Gratitude Quotient (B - A) =

"Practice appreciation for who you are and what you have... and allow your life to unfold in the most amazing way."

- Millen Livis

Day 12 (Evening) Date: Time:

A. How grateful are you right now ? (Use colour pen of your choice and colour the appropriate box)

0	1	2	3	4	5	6	7	8	9	10

Take 3 deep breathes with closed eyes and one hand on your chest and another on your belly.

Now, think of any one thing that you feel grateful about. (You may pick a topic from the prompts given in page 5.) And write at length why you are grateful for this. (put a timer for 5mins)

B. How grateful are you right now ? (Use colour pen of your choice and colour the appropriate box)

0	1	2	3	4	5	6	7	8	9	10

Increase in Gratitude Quotient (B - A) =

"Practice appreciation for who you are and what you have... and allow your life to unfold in the most amazing way."

- Millen Livis

Day 13 (Morning) Date: Time:

A. How grateful are you right now ? (Use a colour pen/pencil of your choice and colour the appropriate box below.

0	1	2	3	4	5	6	7	8	9	10

Do all the exercises below with a broad SMILE on your face.

Close your eyes and scan through your body, mentally - 5 secs.

Open your eyes. Take a coloured pen of your choice and start writing.

I am super excited to start my day because

3 things I feel deeply grateful for, right now, are (write reason as well)

Describe 1 thing from yesterday, that you feel most grateful about Why it is number 1 thing to be grateful about ?

B. How grateful are you right now ?

0	1	2	3	4	5	6	7	8	9	10

Increase in Gratitude Quotient (B - A) =

"When a person doesn't have gratitude, something is missing in his or her humanity."

- Elie Wiesel

Day 13 (Evening) Date: Time:

A. How grateful are you right now ? (Use colour pen of your choice and colour the appropriate box)

0	1	2	3	4	5	6	7	8	9	10

Take 3 deep breathes with closed eyes and one hand on your chest and another on your belly.

Now, think of any one thing that you feel grateful about. (You may pick a topic from the prompts given in page 5.) And write at length why you are grateful for this. (put a timer for 5mins)

B. How grateful are you right now ? (Use colour pen of your choice and colour the appropriate box)

0	1	2	3	4	5	6	7	8	9	10

Increase in Gratitude Quotient (B - A) =

"When a person doesn't have gratitude, something is missing in his or her humanity."

- Elie Wiesel

Day 14 (Morning) Date: Time:

A. How grateful are you right now ? (Use a colour pen/pencil of your choice and colour the appropriate box below.

0	1	2	3	4	5	6	7	8	9	10

Do all the exercises below with a broad SMILE on your face.

Close your eyes and scan through your body, mentally - 5 secs.

Open your eyes. Take a coloured pen of your choice and start writing.

I am super excited to start my day because

3 things I feel deeply grateful for, right now, are (write reason as well)

Describe 1 thing from yesterday, that you feel most grateful about Why it is number 1 thing to be grateful about ?

B. How grateful are you right now ?

0	1	2	3	4	5	6	7	8	9	10

Increase in Gratitude Quotient (B - A) =

"The real gift of gratitude is that the more grateful you are, the more present you become."

- Robert Holden

Day 14 (Evening) Date: Time:

A. How grateful are you right now ? (Use colour pen of your choice and colour the appropriate box)

0	1	2	3	4	5	6	7	8	9	10

Take 3 deep breathes with closed eyes and one hand on your chest and another on your belly.

Now, think of any one thing that you feel grateful about. (You may pick a topic from the prompts given in page 5.) And write at length why you are grateful for this. (put a timer for 5mins)

B. How grateful are you right now ? (Use colour pen of your choice and colour the appropriate box)

0	1	2	3	4	5	6	7	8	9	10

Increase in Gratitude Quotient (B - A) =

"The real gift of gratitude is that the more grateful you are, the more present you become."

- Robert Holden

Day 15 (Morning) Date: Time:

A. How grateful are you right now ? (Use a colour pen/pencil of your choice and colour the appropriate box below.

0	1	2	3	4	5	6	7	8	9	10

Do all the exercises below with a broad SMILE on your face.

Close your eyes and scan through your body, mentally - 5 secs.

Open your eyes. Take a coloured pen of your choice and start writing.

I am super excited to start my day because

3 things I feel deeply grateful for, right now, are (write reason as well)

Describe 1 thing from yesterday, that you feel most grateful about Why it is number 1 thing to be grateful about ?

B. How grateful are you right now ?

0	1	2	3	4	5	6	7	8	9	10

Increase in Gratitude Quotient (B - A) =

"Develop an attitude of gratitude, and give thanks for everything that happens to you, knowing that every step forward is a step toward achieving something bigger and better than your current situation."

- Brian Tracy

Day 15 (Evening) Date: Time:

A. How grateful are you right now ? (Use colour pen of your choice and colour the appropriate box)

0	1	2	3	4	5	6	7	8	9	10

Take 3 deep breathes with closed eyes and one hand on your chest and another on your belly.

Now, think of any one thing that you feel grateful about. (You may pick a topic from the prompts given in page 5.) And write at length why you are grateful for this. (put a timer for 5mins)

B. How grateful are you right now ? (Use colour pen of your choice and colour the appropriate box)

0	1	2	3	4	5	6	7	8	9	10

Increase in Gratitude Quotient (B - A) =

"Develop an attitude of gratitude, and give thanks for everything that happens to you, knowing that every step forward is a step toward achieving something bigger and better than your current situation."

- Brian Tracy

Day 16 (Morning) Date: Time:

A. How grateful are you right now ? (Use a colour pen/pencil of your choice and colour the appropriate box below.

0	1	2	3	4	5	6	7	8	9	10

Do all the exercises below with a broad SMILE on your face.

Close your eyes and scan through your body, mentally - 5 secs.

Open your eyes. Take a coloured pen of your choice and start writing.

I am super excited to start my day because

3 things I feel deeply grateful for, right now, are (write reason as well)

Describe 1 thing from yesterday, that you feel most grateful about Why it is number 1 thing to be grateful about ?

B. How grateful are you right now ?

0	1	2	3	4	5	6	7	8	9	10

Increase in Gratitude Quotient (B - A) =

"I am happy because I'm grateful. I choose to be grateful. That gratitude allows me to be happy."

- Will Arnett

Day 16 (Evening) Date: Time:

A. How grateful are you right now ? (Use colour pen of your choice and colour the appropriate box)

0	1	2	3	4	5	6	7	8	9	10

Take 3 deep breathes with closed eyes and one hand on your chest and another on your belly.

Now, think of any one thing that you feel grateful about. (You may pick a topic from the prompts given in page 5.) And write at length why you are grateful for this. (put a timer for 5mins)

B. How grateful are you right now ? (Use colour pen of your choice and colour the appropriate box)

0	1	2	3	4	5	6	7	8	9	10

Increase in Gratitude Quotient (B - A) =

"I am happy because I'm grateful. I choose to be grateful. That gratitude allows me to be happy."

- Will Arnett

Day 17 (Morning) Date: Time:

A. How grateful are you right now ? (Use a colour pen/pencil of your choice and colour the appropriate box below.

0	1	2	3	4	5	6	7	8	9	10

Do all the exercises below with a broad SMILE on your face.

Close your eyes and scan through your body, mentally - 5 secs.

Open your eyes. Take a coloured pen of your choice and start writing.

I am super excited to start my day because

3 things I feel deeply grateful for, right now, are (write reason as well)

Describe 1 thing from yesterday, that you feel most grateful about Why it is number 1 thing to be grateful about ?

B. How grateful are you right now ?

0	1	2	3	4	5	6	7	8	9	10

Increase in Gratitude Quotient (B - A) =

"If the only prayer you ever say in your entire life is thank you, it will be enough."

- Meister Eckhart

Day 17 (Evening)   Date: Time:

A. How grateful are you right now ? (Use colour pen of your choice and colour the appropriate box)

0	1	2	3	4	5	6	7	8	9	10

Take 3 deep breathes with closed eyes and one hand on your chest and another on your belly.

Now, think of any one thing that you feel grateful about. (You may pick a topic from the prompts given in page 5.) And write at length why you are grateful for this. (put a timer for 5mins)

B. How grateful are you right now ? (Use colour pen of your choice and colour the appropriate box)

0	1	2	3	4	5	6	7	8	9	10

Increase in Gratitude Quotient (B - A) =

"If the only prayer you ever say in your entire life is thank you, it will be enough."

- Meister Eckhart

Day 18 (Morning) Date: Time:

A. How grateful are you right now ? (Use a colour pen/pencil of your choice and colour the appropriate box below.

0	1	2	3	4	5	6	7	8	9	10

Do all the exercises below with a broad SMILE on your face.

Close your eyes and scan through your body, mentally - 5 secs.

Open your eyes. Take a coloured pen of your choice and start writing.

I am super excited to start my day because

3 things I feel deeply grateful for, right now, are (write reason as well)

Describe 1 thing from yesterday, that you feel most grateful about Why it is number 1 thing to be grateful about ?

B. How grateful are you right now ?

0	1	2	3	4	5	6	7	8	9	10

Increase in Gratitude Quotient (B - A) =

"Gratefulness is the key to a happy life that we hold in our hands, because if we are not grateful, then no matter how much we have we will not be happy - because we will always want to have something else or something more."

- David Steindl-Rast

Day 18 (Evening) Date: Time:

A. How grateful are you right now ? (Use colour pen of your choice and colour the appropriate box)

0	1	2	3	4	5	6	7	8	9	10

Take 3 deep breathes with closed eyes and one hand on your chest and another on your belly.

Now, think of any one thing that you feel grateful about. (You may pick a topic from the prompts given in page 5.) And write at length why you are grateful for this. (put a timer for 5mins)

B. How grateful are you right now ? (Use colour pen of your choice and colour the appropriate box)

0	1	2	3	4	5	6	7	8	9	10

Increase in Gratitude Quotient (B - A) =

"Gratefulness is the key to a happy life that we hold in our hands, because if we are not grateful, then no matter how much we have we will not be happy - because we will always want to have something else or something more."

- David Steindl-Rast

Day 19 (Morning) Date: Time:

A. How grateful are you right now ? (Use a colour pen/pencil of your choice and colour the appropriate box below.

0	1	2	3	4	5	6	7	8	9	10

Do all the exercises below with a broad SMILE on your face.

Close your eyes and scan through your body, mentally - 5 secs.

Open your eyes. Take a coloured pen of your choice and start writing.

I am super excited to start my day because

3 things I feel deeply grateful for, right now, are (write reason as well)

Describe 1 thing from yesterday, that you feel most grateful about Why it is number 1 thing to be grateful about ?

B. How grateful are you right now ?

0	1	2	3	4	5	6	7	8	9	10

Increase in Gratitude Quotient (B - A) =

"'Enough' is a feast."

- Buddhist proverb

Day 19 (Evening) Date: Time:

A. How grateful are you right now ? (Use colour pen of your choice and colour the appropriate box)

0	1	2	3	4	5	6	7	8	9	10

Take 3 deep breathes with closed eyes and one hand on your chest and another on your belly.

Now, think of any one thing that you feel grateful about. (You may pick a topic from the prompts given in page 5.) And write at length why you are grateful for this. (put a timer for 5mins)

B. How grateful are you right now ? (Use colour pen of your choice and colour the appropriate box)

0	1	2	3	4	5	6	7	8	9	10

Increase in Gratitude Quotient (B - A) =

"'Enough' is a feast."

- Buddhist proverb

Day 20 (Morning) Date: Time:

A. How grateful are you right now ? (Use a colour pen/pencil of your choice and colour the appropriate box below.

0	1	2	3	4	5	6	7	8	9	10

Do all the exercises below with a broad SMILE on your face.

Close your eyes and scan through your body, mentally - 5 secs.

Open your eyes. Take a coloured pen of your choice and start writing.

I am super excited to start my day because

3 things I feel deeply grateful for, right now, are (write reason as well)

Describe 1 thing from yesterday, that you feel most grateful about Why it is number 1 thing to be grateful about ?

B. How grateful are you right now ?

0	1	2	3	4	5	6	7	8	9	10

Increase in Gratitude Quotient (B - A) =

"When we focus on our gratitude, the tide of disappointment goes out and the tide of love rushes in."

- Kristin Armstrong

Day 20 (Evening) Date: Time:

A. How grateful are you right now ? (Use colour pen of your choice and colour the appropriate box)

0	1	2	3	4	5	6	7	8	9	10

Take 3 deep breathes with closed eyes and one hand on your chest and another on your belly.

Now, think of any one thing that you feel grateful about. (You may pick a topic from the prompts given in page 5.) And write at length why you are grateful for this. (put a timer for 5mins)

B. How grateful are you right now ? (Use colour pen of your choice and colour the appropriate box)

0	1	2	3	4	5	6	7	8	9	10

Increase in Gratitude Quotient (B - A) =

"When we focus on our gratitude, the tide of disappointment goes out and the tide of love rushes in."

- Kristin Armstrong

Day 21 (Morning) Date: Time:

A. How grateful are you right now ? (Use a colour pen/pencil of your choice and colour the appropriate box below.

0	1	2	3	4	5	6	7	8	9	10

Do all the exercises below with a broad SMILE on your face.

Close your eyes and scan through your body, mentally - 5 secs.

Open your eyes. Take a coloured pen of your choice and start writing.

I am super excited to start my day because

3 things I feel deeply grateful for, right now, are (write reason as well)

Describe 1 thing from yesterday, that you feel most grateful about Why it is number 1 thing to be grateful about ?

B. How grateful are you right now ?

0	1	2	3	4	5	6	7	8	9	10

Increase in Gratitude Quotient (B - A) =

"Gratitude is something of which none of us can give too much."

- A. J. Cronin

Day 21 (Evening) Date: Time:

A. How grateful are you right now ? (Use colour pen of your choice and colour the appropriate box)

0	1	2	3	4	5	6	7	8	9	10

Take 3 deep breathes with closed eyes and one hand on your chest and another on your belly.

Now, think of any one thing that you feel grateful about. (You may pick a topic from the prompts given in page 5.) And write at length why you are grateful for this. (put a timer for 5mins)

B. How grateful are you right now ? (Use colour pen of your choice and colour the appropriate box)

0	1	2	3	4	5	6	7	8	9	10

Increase in Gratitude Quotient (B - A) =

"Gratitude is something of which none of us can give too much."

- A. J. Cronin

Day 22 (Morning) Date: Time:

A. How grateful are you right now ? (Use a colour pen/pencil of your choice and colour the appropriate box below.

0	1	2	3	4	5	6	7	8	9	10

Do all the exercises below with a broad SMILE on your face.

Close your eyes and scan through your body, mentally - 5 secs.

Open your eyes. Take a coloured pen of your choice and start writing.

I am super excited to start my day because

3 things I feel deeply grateful for, right now, are (write reason as well)

Describe 1 thing from yesterday, that you feel most grateful about Why it is number 1 thing to be grateful about ?

B. How grateful are you right now ?

0	1	2	3	4	5	6	7	8	9	10

Increase in Gratitude Quotient (B - A) =

"Appreciation is a wonderful thing. It makes what is excellent in others belong to us as well."

- Voltaire

Day 22 (Evening) Date: Time:

A. How grateful are you right now ? (Use colour pen of your choice and colour the appropriate box)

0	1	2	3	4	5	6	7	8	9	10

Take 3 deep breathes with closed eyes and one hand on your chest and another on your belly.

Now, think of any one thing that you feel grateful about. (You may pick a topic from the prompts given in page 5.) And write at length why you are grateful for this. (put a timer for 5mins)

B. How grateful are you right now ? (Use colour pen of your choice and colour the appropriate box)

0	1	2	3	4	5	6	7	8	9	10

Increase in Gratitude Quotient (B - A) =

"Appreciation is a wonderful thing. It makes what is excellent in others belong to us as well."

- Voltaire

Day 23 (Morning) Date: Time:

A. How grateful are you right now ? (Use a colour pen/pencil of your choice and colour the appropriate box below.

0	1	2	3	4	5	6	7	8	9	10

Do all the exercises below with a broad SMILE on your face.

Close your eyes and scan through your body, mentally - 5 secs.

Open your eyes. Take a coloured pen of your choice and start writing.

I am super excited to start my day because

3 things I feel deeply grateful for, right now, are (write reason as well)

Describe 1 thing from yesterday, that you feel most grateful about Why it is number 1 thing to be grateful about ?

B. How grateful are you right now ?

0	1	2	3	4	5	6	7	8	9	10

Increase in Gratitude Quotient (B - A) =

"A grateful heart is a beginning of greatness. It is an expression of humility. It is a foundation for the development of such virtues as prayer, faith, courage, contentment, happiness, love, and well-being."

- James E. Faust

Day 23 (Evening) Date: Time:

A. How grateful are you right now ? (Use colour pen of your choice and colour the appropriate box)

0	1	2	3	4	5	6	7	8	9	10

Take 3 deep breathes with closed eyes and one hand on your chest and another on your belly.

Now, think of any one thing that you feel grateful about. (You may pick a topic from the prompts given in page 5.) And write at length why you are grateful for this. (put a timer for 5mins)

B. How grateful are you right now ? (Use colour pen of your choice and colour the appropriate box)

0	1	2	3	4	5	6	7	8	9	10

Increase in Gratitude Quotient (B - A) =

"A grateful heart is a beginning of greatness. It is an expression of humility. It is a foundation for the development of such virtues as prayer, faith, courage, contentment, happiness, love, and well-being."

- James E. Faust

Day 24 (Morning) Date: Time:

A. How grateful are you right now ? (Use a colour pen/pencil of your choice and colour the appropriate box below.

0	1	2	3	4	5	6	7	8	9	10

Do all the exercises below with a broad SMILE on your face.

Close your eyes and scan through your body, mentally - 5 secs.

Open your eyes. Take a coloured pen of your choice and start writing.

I am super excited to start my day because

3 things I feel deeply grateful for, right now, are (write reason as well)

Describe 1 thing from yesterday, that you feel most grateful about Why it is number 1 thing to be grateful about ?

B. How grateful are you right now ?

0	1	2	3	4	5	6	7	8	9	10

Increase in Gratitude Quotient (B - A) =

"Gratitude opens the door to the power, the wisdom, the creativity of the universe. You open the door through gratitude."

- Deepak Chopra

Day 24 (Evening)   Date: Time:

A. How grateful are you right now ? (Use colour pen of your choice and colour the appropriate box)

0	1	2	3	4	5	6	7	8	9	10

Take 3 deep breathes with closed eyes and one hand on your chest and another on your belly.

Now, think of any one thing that you feel grateful about. (You may pick a topic from the prompts given in page 5.) And write at length why you are grateful for this. (put a timer for 5mins)

B. How grateful are you right now ? (Use colour pen of your choice and colour the appropriate box)

0	1	2	3	4	5	6	7	8	9	10

Increase in Gratitude Quotient (B - A) =

"Gratitude opens the door to the power, the wisdom, the creativity of the universe. You open the door through gratitude."

- Deepak Chopra

Day 25 (Morning) Date: Time:

A. How grateful are you right now ? (Use a colour pen/pencil of your choice and colour the appropriate box below.

0	1	2	3	4	5	6	7	8	9	10

Do all the exercises below with a broad SMILE on your face.

Close your eyes and scan through your body, mentally - 5 secs.

Open your eyes. Take a coloured pen of your choice and start writing.

I am super excited to start my day because

3 things I feel deeply grateful for, right now, are (write reason as well)

Describe 1 thing from yesterday, that you feel most grateful about Why it is number 1 thing to be grateful about ?

B. How grateful are you right now ?

0	1	2	3	4	5	6	7	8	9	10

Increase in Gratitude Quotient (B - A) =

"Gratitude is the wine for the soul. Go on. Get drunk."

- Rumi

Day 25 (Evening) Date: Time:

A. How grateful are you right now ? (Use colour pen of your choice and colour the appropriate box)

0	1	2	3	4	5	6	7	8	9	10

Take 3 deep breathes with closed eyes and one hand on your chest and another on your belly.

Now, think of any one thing that you feel grateful about. (You may pick a topic from the prompts given in page 5.) And write at length why you are grateful for this. (put a timer for 5mins)

B. How grateful are you right now ? (Use colour pen of your choice and colour the appropriate box)

0	1	2	3	4	5	6	7	8	9	10

Increase in Gratitude Quotient (B - A) =

"Gratitude is the wine for the soul. Go on. Get drunk."

- Rumi

Day 26 (Morning) Date: Time:

A. How grateful are you right now ? (Use a colour pen/pencil of your choice and colour the appropriate box below.

0	1	2	3	4	5	6	7	8	9	10

Do all the exercises below with a broad SMILE on your face.

Close your eyes and scan through your body, mentally - 5 secs.

Open your eyes. Take a coloured pen of your choice and start writing.

I am super excited to start my day because

3 things I feel deeply grateful for, right now, are (write reason as well)

Describe 1 thing from yesterday, that you feel most grateful about Why it is number 1 thing to be grateful about ?

B. How grateful are you right now ?

0	1	2	3	4	5	6	7	8	9	10

Increase in Gratitude Quotient (B - A) =

"Imitate until you emulate; match and surpass those who launched you. It's the highest form of thankfulness."

- Mark Victor Hansen

Day 26 (Evening) Date: Time:

A. How grateful are you right now ? (Use colour pen of your choice and colour the appropriate box)

0	1	2	3	4	5	6	7	8	9	10

Take 3 deep breathes with closed eyes and one hand on your chest and another on your belly.

Now, think of any one thing that you feel grateful about. (You may pick a topic from the prompts given in page 5.) And write at length why you are grateful for this. (put a timer for 5mins)

B. How grateful are you right now ? (Use colour pen of your choice and colour the appropriate box)

0	1	2	3	4	5	6	7	8	9	10

Increase in Gratitude Quotient (B - A) =

"Imitate until you emulate; match and surpass those who launched you. It's the highest form of thankfulness."

- Mark Victor Hansen

Day 27 (Morning) Date: Time:

A. How grateful are you right now ? (Use a colour pen/pencil of your choice and colour the appropriate box below.

0	1	2	3	4	5	6	7	8	9	10

Do all the exercises below with a broad SMILE on your face.

Close your eyes and scan through your body, mentally - 5 secs.

Open your eyes. Take a coloured pen of your choice and start writing.

I am super excited to start my day because

3 things I feel deeply grateful for, right now, are (write reason as well)

Describe 1 thing from yesterday, that you feel most grateful about Why it is number 1 thing to be grateful about ?

B. How grateful are you right now ?

0	1	2	3	4	5	6	7	8	9	10

Increase in Gratitude Quotient (B - A) =

"No duty is more urgent than giving thanks."

- James Allen

Day 27 (Evening) Date: Time:

A. How grateful are you right now ? (Use colour pen of your choice and colour the appropriate box)

0	1	2	3	4	5	6	7	8	9	10

Take 3 deep breathes with closed eyes and one hand on your chest and another on your belly.

Now, think of any one thing that you feel grateful about. (You may pick a topic from the prompts given in page 5.) And write at length why you are grateful for this. (put a timer for 5mins)

B. How grateful are you right now ? (Use colour pen of your choice and colour the appropriate box)

0	1	2	3	4	5	6	7	8	9	10

Increase in Gratitude Quotient (B - A) =

"No duty is more urgent than giving thanks."

- James Allen

Day 28 (Morning) Date: Time:

A. How grateful are you right now ? (Use a colour pen/pencil of your choice and colour the appropriate box below.

0	1	2	3	4	5	6	7	8	9	10

Do all the exercises below with a broad SMILE on your face.

Close your eyes and scan through your body, mentally - 5 secs.

Open your eyes. Take a coloured pen of your choice and start writing.

I am super excited to start my day because

3 things I feel deeply grateful for, right now, are (write reason as well)

Describe 1 thing from yesterday, that you feel most grateful about Why it is number 1 thing to be grateful about ?

B. How grateful are you right now ?

0	1	2	3	4	5	6	7	8	9	10

Increase in Gratitude Quotient (B - A) =

"Appreciation in advance brings everything you want to you."

— Esther Hicks

Day 28 (Evening) Date: Time:

A. How grateful are you right now ? (Use colour pen of your choice and colour the appropriate box)

0	1	2	3	4	5	6	7	8	9	10

Take 3 deep breathes with closed eyes and one hand on your chest and another on your belly.

Now, think of any one thing that you feel grateful about. (You may pick a topic from the prompts given in page 5.) And write at length why you are grateful for this. (put a timer for 5mins)

B. How grateful are you right now ? (Use colour pen of your choice and colour the appropriate box)

0	1	2	3	4	5	6	7	8	9	10

Increase in Gratitude Quotient (B - A) =

"Appreciation in advance brings everything you want to you."

— Esther Hicks

Day 29 (Morning) Date: Time:

A. How grateful are you right now ? (Use a colour pen/pencil of your choice and colour the appropriate box below.

0	1	2	3	4	5	6	7	8	9	10

Do all the exercises below with a broad SMILE on your face.

Close your eyes and scan through your body, mentally - 5 secs.

Open your eyes. Take a coloured pen of your choice and start writing.

I am super excited to start my day because

3 things I feel deeply grateful for, right now, are (write reason as well)

Describe 1 thing from yesterday, that you feel most grateful about Why it is number 1 thing to be grateful about ?

B. How grateful are you right now ?

0	1	2	3	4	5	6	7	8	9	10

Increase in Gratitude Quotient (B - A) =

"When I started counting my blessings, my whole life turned around."

- Willie Nelson

Day 29 (Evening) Date: Time:

A. How grateful are you right now ? (Use colour pen of your choice and colour the appropriate box)

0	1	2	3	4	5	6	7	8	9	10

Take 3 deep breathes with closed eyes and one hand on your chest and another on your belly.

Now, think of any one thing that you feel grateful about. (You may pick a topic from the prompts given in page 5.) And write at length why you are grateful for this. (put a timer for 5mins)

B. How grateful are you right now ? (Use colour pen of your choice and colour the appropriate box)

0	1	2	3	4	5	6	7	8	9	10

Increase in Gratitude Quotient (B - A) =

"When I started counting my blessings, my whole life turned around."

- Willie Nelson

Day 30 (Morning) Date: Time:

A. How grateful are you right now ? (Use a colour pen/pencil of your choice and colour the appropriate box below.

0	1	2	3	4	5	6	7	8	9	10

Do all the exercises below with a broad SMILE on your face.

Close your eyes and scan through your body, mentally - 5 secs.

Open your eyes. Take a coloured pen of your choice and start writing.

I am super excited to start my day because

3 things I feel deeply grateful for, right now, are (write reason as well)

Describe 1 thing from yesterday, that you feel most grateful about Why it is number 1 thing to be grateful about ?

B. How grateful are you right now ?

0	1	2	3	4	5	6	7	8	9	10

Increase in Gratitude Quotient (B - A) =

"A grateful mindset can set you free from the prison of disempowerment and the shackles of misery."

- Steve Maraboli

Day 30 (Evening) Date: Time:

A. How grateful are you right now ? (Use colour pen of your choice and colour the appropriate box)

0	1	2	3	4	5	6	7	8	9	10

Take 3 deep breathes with closed eyes and one hand on your chest and another on your belly.

Now, think of any one thing that you feel grateful about. (You may pick a topic from the prompts given in page 5.) And write at length why you are grateful for this. (put a timer for 5mins)

B. How grateful are you right now ? (Use colour pen of your choice and colour the appropriate box)

0	1	2	3	4	5	6	7	8	9	10

Increase in Gratitude Quotient (B - A) =

"A grateful mindset can set you free from the prison of disempowerment and the shackles of misery."

- Steve Maraboli

Day (Morning) Date: Time:

A. How grateful are you right now ? (Use a colour pen/pencil of your choice and colour the appropriate box below.

0	1	2	3	4	5	6	7	8	9	10

Do all the exercises below with a broad SMILE on your face.

Close your eyes and scan through your body, mentally - 5 secs.

Open your eyes. Take a coloured pen of your choice and start writing.

I am super excited to start my day because

3 things I feel deeply grateful for, right now, are (write reason as well)

Describe 1 thing from yesterday, that you feel most grateful about Why it is number 1 thing to be grateful about ?

B. How grateful are you right now ?

0	1	2	3	4	5	6	7	8	9	10

Increase in Gratitude Quotient (B - A) =

"Gratitude is an opener of locked-up blessings."

- Marianne Williamson

Day (Evening) Date: Time:

A. How grateful are you right now ? (Use colour pen of your choice and colour the appropriate box)

0	1	2	3	4	5	6	7	8	9	10

Take 3 deep breathes with closed eyes and one hand on your chest and another on your belly.

Now, think of any one thing that you feel grateful about. (You may pick a topic from the prompts given in page 5.) And write at length why you are grateful for this. (put a timer for 5mins)

B. How grateful are you right now ? (Use colour pen of your choice and colour the appropriate box)

0	1	2	3	4	5	6	7	8	9	10

Increase in Gratitude Quotient (B - A) =

"Gratitude is an opener of locked-up blessings."

- Marianne Williamson

Day (Morning) Date: Time:

A. How grateful are you right now ? (Use a colour pen/pencil of your choice and colour the appropriate box below.

0	1	2	3	4	5	6	7	8	9	10

Do all the exercises below with a broad SMILE on your face.

Close your eyes and scan through your body, mentally - 5 secs.

Open your eyes. Take a coloured pen of your choice and start writing.

I am super excited to start my day because

3 things I feel deeply grateful for, right now, are (write reason as well)

Describe 1 thing from yesterday, that you feel most grateful about Why it is number 1 thing to be grateful about ?

B. How grateful are you right now ?

0	1	2	3	4	5	6	7	8	9	10

Increase in Gratitude Quotient (B - A) =

"Gratitude is the sign of noble souls."

- Aesop

Day (Evening) Date: Time:

A. How grateful are you right now ? (Use colour pen of your choice and colour the appropriate box)

0	1	2	3	4	5	6	7	8	9	10

Take 3 deep breathes with closed eyes and one hand on your chest and another on your belly.

Now, think of any one thing that you feel grateful about. (You may pick a topic from the prompts given in page 5.) And write at length why you are grateful for this. (put a timer for 5mins)

B. How grateful are you right now ? (Use colour pen of your choice and colour the appropriate box)

0	1	2	3	4	5	6	7	8	9	10

Increase in Gratitude Quotient (B - A) =

"Gratitude is the sign of noble souls."

- Aesop

Day (Morning) Date: Time:

A. How grateful are you right now ? (Use a colour pen/pencil of your choice and colour the appropriate box below.

0	1	2	3	4	5	6	7	8	9	10

Do all the exercises below with a broad SMILE on your face.

Close your eyes and scan through your body, mentally - 5 secs.

Open your eyes. Take a coloured pen of your choice and start writing.

I am super excited to start my day because

3 things I feel deeply grateful for, right now, are (write reason as well)

Describe 1 thing from yesterday, that you feel most grateful about Why it is number 1 thing to be grateful about ?

B. How grateful are you right now ?

0	1	2	3	4	5	6	7	8	9	10

Increase in Gratitude Quotient (B - A) =

"When you are grateful, fear disappears and abundance appears."

- Anthony Robbins

Day (Evening) Date: Time:

A. How grateful are you right now ? (Use colour pen of your choice and colour the appropriate box)

0	1	2	3	4	5	6	7	8	9	10

Take 3 deep breathes with closed eyes and one hand on your chest and another on your belly.

Now, think of any one thing that you feel grateful about. (You may pick a topic from the prompts given in page 5.) And write at length why you are grateful for this. (put a timer for 5mins)

B. How grateful are you right now ? (Use colour pen of your choice and colour the appropriate box)

0	1	2	3	4	5	6	7	8	9	10

Increase in Gratitude Quotient (B - A) =

"When you are grateful, fear disappears and abundance appears."

- Anthony Robbins

Thank you (Use any prompt)

Thank you (Use any prompt)

Thank you (Use any prompt)

Thank you (Use any prompt)

Thank you (Use any prompt)

When life is a game ,
GRATITUDE is a game changer.
- Uma Srikar

www.ingramcontent.com/pod-product-compliance
Lightning Source LLC
LaVergne TN
LVHW021137160826
845679LV00023B/1947
* 9 7 9 8 8 9 1 8 6 2 2 6 5 *